Leaving

and

Entering

Kenneth L. Sturgill

ISBN: 1451562985

EAN: 13-9781451562989

Printed by CreateSpace

Publisher:
Apostle Kenneth L. Sturgill
ksturgill@comcast.net

Contents

Forward

Kenneth Sturgill has written a profound, philosophical presentation of God's requirements to live a successful life. His writing style provokes productive self-analysis. This book will inspire you to succeed by properly leaving your failures behind.

Karl D. Coke, PhD
Karl Coke Evangelistic Association
Charlotte, NC

Preface

Leaving and Entering by Apostle/Pastor Kenneth L. Sturgill is a freeing, life-changing book that every Christian should read over and over and apply day by day to each relationship and situation.

His insight into appropriately leaving one season, with no strings attached, and appropriately entering the next season, frees people to live more abundantly. What is a season? It could be as simple as washing all the dishes of a meal in order to leave the meal season properly and enjoy with abundance the next event or season of the day. Or it could be as complex as leaving a church correctly, with no lingering bitterness over past situations so as to enter correctly into the next season in the Body of Christ.

His insight into the process of forgiveness by Enforcing the Victory of the Cross brings a greater depth of freedom from past words or situations that may have damaged us. This process is revolutionary and can be applied in minor situations, daily, as well as extreme situations on occasion. If you still struggle to gain freedom in any area of your life, there could be a hidden need to Enforce the Victory of the Cross, even though forgiveness has been given as much as possible.

It is essential for you to Leave and Enter in peace according to the will of God.

It has been an extremely great pleasure and labor of love to assist with the publishing of these important words about *Leaving and Entering*. These teachings and scriptures will influence all persons reading this book. As they learn to apply these principles to their lives, they will walk successfully in their God-given assignment.

We have experienced the great love and devotion for God by Apostles Kenneth L. and Phyllis Sturgill as we helped develop this great book!

Rev. Dr. Stanley B. and Nancy Patterson
New Beginnings Ministry
Salem, SC

Acknowledgements

I want to thank my wife, Phyllis, for her unselfish love. I have spent many hours writing and preparing this book and the beginning chapters of two other books. She has been an encourager and a motivator for me to write. Her prayers and prophetic words have been much help and strength to me. Phyllis has stood with me and together we have weathered storms of new beginnings many times. Thank you my darlin', Phyllis, for all your help and support.

Thanks to my church family who accepted the Principles of Leaving and Entering as we journeyed through seasons of change. Their acceptance of me as an apostle, on the cutting edge of what God is saying now, has led us through many transitions of restored truth for the body of Christ.

Stan and Nancy Patterson, you were my "ram in the bush." You were a divine connection from God to help me with editing and formatting this book. You have spent many hours, and I appreciate every moment you gave to help me. Thanks to both of you for your love.

Thank you Joyce Jones, my typist, for taking my messy scribbled notes and typing them for me. Only you can decipher them. You are a blessing.

I want to thank my assistant Pastor Rick Smith. Before I left for vacation last fall, Rick brought me a special notebook and prophesied to me to work on the book. While on the airplane the introduction for the book was written as the Holy Spirit gave it to me.

Special thanks to Melissa Fields of Don Fields Photography in Sevierville, TN. She and her husband Don currently are serving as president of Tennessee Photography Association. Melissa finished the book cover with the beautiful picture leaving the past and entering the glory of the future.

My special thanks go to the late Dr. Fuchsia Pickett, my Mother in the Lord. She was a great mentor to me. While at lunch with her, she leaned toward me, pointed her finger at me and said, "Write the book." At that time, I was only teaching the principles of Leaving and Entering. She told me to hurry because she wanted to endorse the book for me. I did not finish this book before her homecoming, but Thank You Dr. Pickett for your encouragement, impartation and confidence in me.

Introduction

A question that haunts many and torments the mind is "Why has life dealt me such a bad blow?" This happens because we do not follow the patterns of God. One of the most important patterns we need to learn is the pattern of "Leaving and Entering."

Life is filled with seasons, beginnings and endings. These times and seasons must have a correct beginning and a correct ending. We often hear the phrase "We have entered the beginning of the end." This phrase is not entirely a true or accurate concept. If the beginning is not from truth and accurate, then there can be multiple endings. If the beginning is incorrect, the completion cannot be correct.

The Bible says in Matthew 7:13-14 there are two roads. One road is narrow and leads to life, and the other road is broad and leads to destruction. These roads run parallel to each other and lead us to our final destination of heaven or hell. These roads lead us in our journey through life, the life that God planned for us.

We must choose which one we want to travel. On this journey, God has planned many times and seasons for us to encounter. When we exit from the narrow road to the broad road, we have made an illegal exit (leaving) and an illegal entrance (entering) onto the new road. In order to get back on the narrow road, a correction must be made. The first step is to stop and repent.

Repentance is turning from one direction and going in another direction. We must exit (leave) the broad road and make an entrance (enter) into the narrow road. The time and distance we were on the broad road cannot be retrieved or restored. This is lost. It is gone. What you could have done or could have experienced is lost.

Once we get back on the narrow road, there is a reaping process we must go through because of our failure. The false exit (leaving) wasn't planned and neither was the false **entrance (entering) because they did not originate from God**. When a beginning does not originate from God or was not planned by God, then the false beginning must be ended so that one can again travel on the narrow way.

The same principle can be applied to times and seasons that are planned by God in our journey through life. There is a true beginning of a season and a true ending of a season. If we do not leave a season on time, then we cannot be on time to enter the new season because we are out of time and out of unity with God's purpose.

The Bible tells us,

For every purpose and matter has its right time and judgment... Ecclesiastes 8:6 (Amp)

Also, bunny trails can lead us off the narrow road by taking us in circles instead of crossing over to the broad road. Bunny trails are non-destiny activities and non-destiny relationships.

non-destiny activities
non-destiny relationships

They create false beginnings which will alter our destiny, but not to the point of crossing to the broad road. Unless these false beginnings are brought to an end, we will never reach our full potential.

Abraham, Ishmael and Isaac are biblical examples of this process. Abraham created a wrong beginning in Ishmael, mocking the true beginning in Isaac. God told Abraham to remove Ishmael (the false beginning) from their midst. A true ending can be completed only if the beginning originated from the source of truth.

Before the beginning of time, God knew our end and had a plan for our lives (Isaiah 46:9-10). So God desires to bring true endings to all things and to all false beginnings. The true ending is your potential and everyone has potential to fulfill God's plan. However, unless the beginning is from God, the Creator of the universe, there can be many false endings. God preordained the beginning of all things (Ephesians 1:4-5,11). Therefore, if the beginning of anything in your life is not part of your predestined purpose and destiny, it has to be brought to an end for you to be successful and prosperous. The true ending comes when purpose is achieved.

God is the source of truth. Unless the beginning originates from Him, everything else is a lie. God has given His divine plan for our lives. When we find His patterns and apply the principles of those patterns, we will be successful. He also delights in the prosperity of His people (Psalm 35:27), so why do we live in the hit and miss, trial and error methods when He has provided a way for our steps throughout life.

There are always conflicts or struggles between spirit and flesh. As long as we are trying to push ahead when God is trying to end a false beginning, there will be struggles, disappointments, troubles and little joy. Jeremiah 29:11 tells us He has made provision for our success through

His Word and when we find the principles of truth and apply them, we can be set free.

And you shall know the truth and the truth will make you free. John 8: 32

We must bring proper closures to be on time for true beginnings.

Is 46:9 Remember the former things of old: for I Am God and there is none else; I Am God and there is none like me. Is 46:10 Declaring the end from the beginning, and from ancient times the things that are not yet done, saying My counsel shall stand, and I will do all my pleasure.

Eph 1:11 In whom Also we have obtained an inheritance, being predistinated according to the purpose of him who worketh all things after the Counsel of his own will.

Ps 35:27 ... Let the Lord be magnified, which hath pleasure in the prosperity of his servant.

Jer 29:11 For I know the thoughts that I think toward you, saith the Lord, thoughts of peace, and not of evil, to give you an expected end.

Part One

Leaving

Ecc 3:1 To every thing there is a season, and a time to every purpose under the heaven

Gen 1:1 In the beginning God created the heaven and the earth.

Chapter One

Overview – Leaving and Entering

Down through the ages, an often asked question has been "Which comes first, the chicken or the egg?" The different views and arguments depend on whether you are a creationist or an evolutionist. It is much easier to believe in a divine Creator than to believe everything evolved from a tiny cell or big bang theory. The chicken came first because God created all the animals on the fifth day of creation. Man is such a highly developed, complicated, detailed being, he could not have just happened. God in His omniscient wisdom planned everything, then created it with His power and placed all future happenings in times and seasons (Ecclesiastes 3:1).

Which comes first, leaving or entering? In the beginning God created the heaven and the earth (Genesis 1:1). God created man and placed him in the Garden of Eden in the beginning, so the beginning is the entering. Beginnings determine endings. Adam and Eve entered the garden and so began the pattern of Entering and Leaving.

9

Beginnings
determine endings

The first beginning became the first Principle of Entering. God told Adam he could eat of every tree in the garden, except the tree of the knowledge of good and evil. Adam did not follow the instructions of God, his Creator, and therefore entered incorrectly. Because of this, he was removed and banned from the garden. This started the Principle of Leaving. Because Adam left man in a fallen state with this pattern, we must apply the Principle of Leaving (the fallen state) before we can enter properly. If we do not leave correctly, then we cannot enter correctly.

The past pulls on us like a gigantic rubber band and will allow us to go only so far; then it pulls us back into the same old habits, limitations, and patterns. We will continue the same old struggles of life until we can leave correctly by the Principles of Leaving. Let me say that again. If old habits keep coming back, perhaps you have not left a season correctly.

Do we want to achieve a successful, happy and prosperous life and arrive at our planned destiny and the end that God has planned for us? If we do, then we have to reenter the Garden and complete our purpose in life by following the Principles of Leaving and Entering. Leaving and

10

Entering is the first and most important pattern that God gave man to follow. This pattern is all through the Bible and is essential for our success.

II Cor 5:18 And all things are of God, who hath
reconciled us to himself by Jesus Christ, and
hath given to us the ministry of reconciliation

Chapter Two

Principle I – The Redemptive Process

II Corinthians 5:18 - God reconciled us back to Him.

Leaving and Entering are the main Principles of life. Leaving is the first step we must take because Adam sinned when he disobeyed God and caused the fall of man. God removed Adam and Eve from the Garden and His presence, and man found himself separated from God. Then he became a servant of Satan. Man gave his crown of authority to Satan and gave Satan the right to become "god of this world." This activated the kingdom of darkness and the soulish realm of man. God, out of His love and mercy, initiated His redemptive plan for man. This redemptive process was done in stages which God introduced as times and seasons. This will be discussed in a later chapter.

The redemptive process took place so God could teach man that He was in control, and the earth is His Kingdom and His rule. Because man's spirit desired a relationship with God, the Creator, he started his soulish search to reach God and

13

become His son and servant again. This happened simultaneously with God's redemptive plan for man. This started the war and struggle inside of man. Will the soul of man win or will the spirit of man win the battle?

The soul of man is the self life of mind, emotion, and will. The spirit of man is the life of God in us and is faith and love. This struggle produced religion, which is man's system of finding God and serving Him. Religion is a false beginning. A true beginning has to come from the seed of God and not from the seed of man. Religion causes a false leaving by man because of his relationship with Satan. Religion has its roots in the world's system and is influenced by the kingdom of darkness. Religion is like the tower of Babel. It is man's way to reach into the heavens to find God by man's own concepts, counsel, theories, ideas, and opinions.

Religion is not God's heart or His plans, principles, truth, or laws; therefore, religion cannot successfully leave the bondage of Satan and his kingdom of darkness. Religion is a highly thought out, organized plan of Satan to deceive many. The purpose of this plan of deception is to confuse man into thinking he has successfully left the kingdom of darkness.

Religion
deceives man into thinking
he has left the kingdom of darkness

Because we have not successfully left the kingdom of darkness, we have not fully entered into God's Kingdom and all His provisions for us.

A religious spirit will cause us
to desire a denomination
or a false religion
more than an encounter with Truth

A man has to have a desire for truth and know truth in order to be free. Unless we have a desire for truth, we will remain blinded, captivated and in bondage to religion.

The redemptive process of God is God's plan to restore man back to a relationship with Him, as He had with Adam. God desires man to return to the Garden provided for him and enter into His rest of complete *freedom, peace, rule, dominion, authority,* and *victory.* The redemptive process is salvation which is defined as deliverance. God wants to completely deliver us from evil and Satan's snare so we can walk away from serving the devil and start serving God.

15

God gave man a pattern and example of how to serve Him and please Him in the giving of the tabernacle. God divided the tabernacle into three sections: *1. Outer Court 2. Inner Court 3. Holy of Holies.* God established this pattern to have different rules and principles to follow in each individual section. We determine which level of relationship with God we have by the lifestyle we live and the rules and principles we obey.

All those who do not acknowledge that God Jehovah is the only true and sovereign God are living outside the tabernacle. Those who serve other gods (idols) and religions do not have a relationship with God. Adam experienced this when he did not acknowledge God as sovereign and was removed from the Garden (from the presence and relationship with God).

The *Outer Court* is for those who practice rituals and sacrifices. The *Inner Court* represents the symbols of God. Symbols are a substitute for the real thing. The *Inner Court* is for those in a maturing relationship with God. They serve God in ministry not knowing there is more to come. The shewbread was made by man and remained for seven days. However, God wants to give us His daily bread of purpose and provision, not bread that lasts seven days. The lampstand or menorah is also a small light compared to the Glory of God. The altar of incense behind the curtain is for the compromised, unholy, ungodly lifestyle that we live. This fragrance of compromise we create does not please God.

The *Holy of Holies* is the place where God dwells. This is the place where He desires man to abide with Him in an intimate relationship. This is the place of God's presence. It is the place to receive our daily bread from Him, a place of the true light of God that will cause us to radiate His light to a dark world. Our pure worship at His feet creates a true incense and is evidence of His character manifested in us.

The prophet Elijah asked the Israelites, "Are you going to serve Baal or are you going to serve God?" This is also our choice. Do you want to live the cursed lifestyle of the first Adam or do you want to have the blessings of life of the second Adam, the Lord Jesus Christ? Do you want truth and life in the *Holy of Holies* with all the covenant blessings, or do you want to continue to live a life of lies, deception, and religious activities of man causing you to reap and suffer God's wrath?

Chapter Three

Principle II – Acknowledge God's Sovereignty

Revelation 22:12 & 13 - I am Alpha and Omega.

Failing to honor God as the beginning of all things and the end of all things will result in the loss of the best that God has planned for our lives. It will cause us to suffer eternal torment at the end of time. We have to acknowledge that God is the Most High God. He is the Supreme Being and Creator of Heaven and Earth. He alone is God and everything else is an idol created by man's own imagination and creativity. Man in his search for significance, identity, purpose and tranquility has created false gods.

Some people even have the audacity to exalt themselves as god. This follows the same pattern established by Adam, the first man. We need to wake up, shake ourselves, look at what happened to Adam, and abandon this pattern of establishing ourselves as god by doing as we please. This principle caused Adam to live outside the realm of true victory and peace, outside the realm of the

19

Kingdom of God where everything was planned and established for him to enjoy life at its fullness.

Man is still living outside the Garden because he does not follow the pattern of Leaving and Entering. Adam disobeyed God's first and second commands. God told Adam not to eat from the Tree of Knowledge of good and evil. God's second command to Adam was to eat from the Tree of Life (Genesis 2:16-17). Adam disobeyed both of those commandments. Today we are still disobeying the two commandments of God.

> **You shall love the Lord your God with all your heart, and the second is like it, you shall love your neighbor as yourself.**
> Matthew 22:37-39

When we have a new beginning (Entering) outside of what God has planned, we are no different than Adam. We will suffer the same consequences. God will have to bring our wrong path to an end to get us back on track to His planned purpose for our lives. Do we want to live outside of God's best for us, His fullness for us? We have the ability of choice, but we do not have the right of choice outside of God's plan for our lives. Man has to take a close look at what Adam did and what he reaped. He lost the Kingdom of God because he disobeyed. The second Principle of Leaving is to acknowledge God as sovereign.

The second Principle of Leaving is to acknowledge God is sovereign

It is God's Kingdom, and He is King over it. We are His planned family. He has planned our lives, our purposes, our gifts and callings, our motives, when we are to be born, and where we are to live and go to church. When we realize He is God, and we are not our own, then we can submit to His principles, laws and rules. It is then and only then that we can leave the pattern Adam set in motion because of his failure to acknowledge God and His authority.

For we must all appear before the judgment seat of Christ, that each one may receive the things done in the body, according to what he has done, whether good or bad.

II Corinthians 5:10

Not only do we suffer in this life for our failures, but we will suffer in a never ending future of torment in the lake of fire.

And anyone not found written in the Book of Life was cast into the lake of fire.

Revelation 20:15

But the cowardly, unbelieving, abominable, murderers, sexually immoral, sorcerers, idolaters, and all liars shall have their

21

part in the lake which burns with fire and brimstone, which is the second death.

Revelation 21:8

What do you think of the sovereignty of God? How do your actions line up with what you think? When we doubt the sovereignty of God, we are following the pattern of the fallen Adam.

Chapter Four

Principle III - Forgiveness

*Forgiveness means
to release one's sins from the sinner.
Forgiveness means freedom, pardon, and
denotes a release from bondage or imprisonment.*

Forgiveness is from the root word "to forgive" which means to send forth, to send away or let go. Firstly, it signifies the remission of the punishment due to sinful conduct. Secondly, it involves the complete removal of the cause of offense. Jesus emphasizes the importance of forgiveness in making it a part of the Lord's Prayer. He tells us that if we do not forgive others, He will not forgive us.

And forgive us our debts, as we forgive our debtors. Matthew 6:12

14For if ye forgive men their trespasses, your heavenly Father will also forgive you: 15But if ye forgive not men their trespasses, neither will your Father forgive your trespasses.
Matthew 6:14-15

The first step in forgiveness is repentance. We cannot truly forgive without a contrite heart and the brokenness of our soul. We become willing in our hearts to release and send away the offense.

As individuals, we repent for our failure to acknowledge the sovereignty of God, for disobeying His laws and principles, for listening and yielding ourselves to the kingdom of darkness, and for being seduced to serve the devil as Adam did. We cut the umbilical cord attached to the devil when we repent. This is the cord of sin that binds us and keeps us connected to the kingdom of darkness. When we yield ourselves to serve the devil, then we become his servants.

Do you not know that to whom you present yourselves slaves to obey, you are that one's slaves whom you obey, whether of sin leading to death, or of obedience leading to righteousness? Romans 6:16

His life of evil is connected to us and is giving us a flow of his blood life of sin and immorality. It becomes your life source.

Principle III – Forgiveness

You become
what you are connected to

Jesus said if we do not forgive others, He will not forgive us (Matthew 6:14-15). Why is this? He cannot forgive us if we are still connected to Satan. In the spirit realm, the devil is our father until we sever the cord from him.

Repentance is more than turning and going in a different direction. Repentance takes away the legal right of the spiritual kingdom of darkness to remain. It is cutting away the cord, stopping the flow, pull, and influence of darkness on our lives. It is trading families. It is changing allegiance from Satan to God. This is why we need true repentance.

True repentance is more than confession with our mouth. **True repentance is allowing the sword of the spirit to cut the cord of life support from Satan.** It is an experience with the Holy Spirit. The pattern of the prodigal son, before he could enter into the Kingdom of the Father, was for him to ask for forgiveness. Then God restored all to him.

Repentance will cause you to turn and walk away from situations, circumstances, and your past. This enables you to leave correctly and qualifies you to enter your future destiny. The prodigal son left the hog pen, the life of sin, and entered into a new life of provision in his Father's house.

The second step of forgiveness is following the example of Jesus when He died on the cross. It also involves the complete removal of the cause of the offense. As I was hungry to know Jesus intimately, pushing forward to develop a deeper relationship with Him, He spoke these words to me, "**Enforce the Victory of the Cross.**"

These words resonated in me for days. They were like a recording playing over and over inside me. I sought God about it, and prayed and prayed, asking Him what He was saying. I thought I was already enforcing the victory of the cross. I thought I was teaching forgiveness and walking in forgiveness.

At this point, my wife and I began a journey that brought us to a new realm of understanding. The Holy Spirit led us into a deliverance ministry. We knew very little about deliverance and the steps needed to set people free from the attacks of the enemy and influence of evil spirits. The Lord first took both of us through a *process of forgiveness and healing,* setting us free from the bondages the past had dealt to us. The Holy Spirit led us into steps and certain principles to follow to set people free. Forgiveness is step number one.

Out of this *process*, God gave me a revelation of how to forgive. As I heard His instructions step by step, I suddenly realized that I only knew the first part of forgiveness which is repentance (asking God to forgive). I had never been taught or read what the Holy Spirit spoke to me. This was exciting to me and made me want to take everyone through the *process of forgiveness*. Look at Hosea Chapter 4.

My people are destroyed for lack of knowledge: because thou hast rejected knowledge, I will also reject thee, that thou shalt be no priest to me: seeing thou hast forgotten the law of thy God, I will also forget thy children. Hosea 4:6

The definition of "destroyed" in this scripture is "to be silent, to destroy, to perish." The definition of "reject" in each instance is "to run away, to disappear, to reject, to refuse." God is saying here that He will be silent and run away from us. We will not be able to see His glory or hear His voice. When we do not have an understanding of His law, we cannot reap the benefits the law provides.

This is one reason many never completely walk in the full benefits of forgiveness. We need a full understanding of the *process of forgiveness*. Because we have partial understanding of forgiveness, we are still harboring a degree of unforgive-

27

ness. **Where there is unforgiveness, there is the potential of attack from the devil.** We say we have forgiven, but then out of nowhere the devil comes with thoughts or feelings of unforgiveness, anger, bitterness, and a desire to avoid the situation or persons involved. We stand back and wonder where these things came from.

> **And ye shall know the truth, and the truth shall make you free.** John 8:32

If we only know part of a truth, we cannot reap the fullness of that truth. When we leave a season or a situation, we want to leave totally free. We want to leave the past with no attachments. **We want to walk out of the darkness of the old and into the light of the new.**

The Holy Spirit gave a vision of a completed puzzle and gave me the understanding of each piece. **The first piece of the picture** the Lord spoke to me is "**As long as there is unforgiveness, known or unknown, the devil can attack.**"

Unforgiveness is like giving the devil a key to your house so he can come and go as he pleases. Jesus describes the devil as a thief, and we need to regulate him to this role. You have legal rights and authority over a thief, but who can control someone who has a key to your house? As a thief or a trespasser, you can punish him, regulate him, dictate to him, control him, and make him obey you. However, if you give him a key, you can do none of these. He becomes a guest in your house.

The second piece of the picture came when I asked the Holy Spirit, "How do we give the devil a key to our house?" He said, "**The key is guilt**." When an offense is committed, someone's rights have been violated. Someone has to assume that guilt whether guilty or not. This guilt still links you to the situation and leaves the door open for the devil. Jesus took the guilt on the cross although He was not guilty of anything.

> **Who did no sin, neither was guile found in his mouth:** 1 Peter 2:21-22

As part of forgiveness Jesus took our guilt and our sin upon Himself, took it to the cross, and defeated the devil. He stripped the devil of the legal right to attack us. Jesus took the keys of death and hell from him.

The third piece of the picture came when the Holy Spirit again said to me, "**Enforce the Victory of the Cross**." He said to look at Jesus' example of dying on the cross. I did this for several days and then it was like an explosion went off inside me. I saw it! I suddenly had the full understanding of what he was showing me about forgiveness.

Let's picture the guilt and blame as a basketball. When two people are in disagreement or an offense is committed, no one wants to take the basketball. The basketball is tossed back and forth between the parties involved with no one to assume the guilt. One says, "I am not guilty" and tosses the ball to the other; then it's tossed back saying, "I am not guilty." Passing the ball back and forth can go on forever, and the devil is laughing all the while. So when we use Jesus' example of taking upon ourselves the guilt and blame, taking it to the cross even though we are not guilty, leaving it there, and covering it with the blood of Jesus, we make a way for Holy Spirit to resolve the issues of everyone involved.

The fourth piece of the picture is confess with your mouth the victory of Jesus over guilt and blame. Decree and declare the defeat of the devil as Jesus defeated the devil at the cross. Jesus stripped the devil of his authority and reconciled man to God.

Principle III – Forgiveness

Six things take place when we follow Jesus' Pattern:

1. It removes the guilt and blame which divides the parties involved.

2. It brings reconciliation

3. Unforgiveness is totally removed by the blood of Jesus

4. We take the keys back from the devil as Jesus did.

5. The blessings and favor of God can now rest upon all involved.

6. The devil has to return everything he has stolen and pay a fine of seven times over.

But if he be found, he shall restore sevenfold; he shall give all the substance of his house. Proverbs 6:31

We have seen many relationships and families restored, money restored, possessions and jobs restored through this process. God refers to our forefathers, Abraham, Isaac and Jacob as our examples. Jacob, by forgiving his father-in-law Laban, successfully cut the past from him and established a barrier between himself and Laban, who was his enemy. Jacob built a memorial of stone to serve as a barrier separating him from

31

Laban. This also served as a reminder for Jacob not to return to the old lifestyle of serving Laban. He would now serve God. This barrier also served as a reminder to Laban not to cross and pursue Jacob. Forgiveness provides a spiritual barrier to keep Satan from having a key to pursue us.

Forgiveness closes the door

When we close the door of the past and place a barrier, a memorial, or a covenant that we will not return, this stops the devil from crossing to you, and it keeps you from crossing to him. You see yourself (without vision we perish) entering a new door and closing the door of the past.

Here is an example of applying the *process of forgiveness.* A man called me for an appointment for marriage counseling and prayer. At the start of the interview he broke down and started crying. He was distraught and really broken when he told me his wife had left him for sexual relations with other men. In an interview I tried to get to the root of the problem because if you deal only with the surface of the issues, you will not have complete success. So I started to ask questions, trying to lead him into telling me the process leading up to his wife leaving him. He assured me he had done nothing to provoke her actions. He told her he loved her, he bought her gifts, he remembered all the important calendar dates, he never abused her in any way, and he sexually pleased her. After questioning him in all the surface and deep, intimate details of his marriage and by the leading of the Holy Spirit, I came to the conclusion that he was telling the truth.

I asked him what he was willing to do to get his wife back. He said he was willing to do anything. After instructing him on the principles of forgiveness, I explained what the Lord had shown me about enforcing the victory of the cross. In this case it meant never remembering what she had done, never bringing up her leaving him, never asking her about the men or sexual encounters and showing her more affection and love than he had before. He agreed; then he was ready for the second part of forgiveness. Even though he was not guilty of anything that led her to leave him, he was willing to take all the guilt and blame upon himself and take it to the cross. Jesus gave us this pattern to totally defeat the devil.

He prayed the prayer of forgiveness, and I agreed with him. About two weeks later he called me and said he and his wife were reconciling their marriage. He wanted me to talk and pray with both of them. The principles that Jesus left us work if we are willing to follow them. Hallelujah!

On another occasion, we took a young man through the *process of forgiveness* to remove anger and unforgiveness toward his dad. His dad had left him and his mother when he was young. He grew up not experiencing the love and care of a father. At first he was bitter and angry at his dad, but as he grew older, he tried to forgive him. The young man wanted to see his dad, but did not know where he was. After we took him through the *full process of forgiveness,* his dad called him and wanted to meet him. We have many more accounts of God restoring relationships and working miracles out of seemingly hopeless situations.

Prayer of Forgiveness

Heavenly Father I come to you now in the Name of Jesus and I choose to forgive _____ for_____.

I take the guilt and blame as You did, Jesus. I take it upon myself and take it to the cross. I leave it there and cover it with the blood of Jesus. Now Satan, you are defeated and I loose everyone involved. I demand everything you've taken to be returned seven times over. I take the key of guilt from you. You no longer have a key to my house. I relegate you as a trespasser and a thief. I am free in Jesus name. Amen

Steps in the *Process of Forgiveness*

1. Repent for our failure to acknowledge the sovereignty of God, for disobeying His laws and principles, for listening and yielding ourselves to the kingdom of darkness, and for being seduced to serve the devil as Adam did.

2. Follow the example of Jesus when He died on the cross, including the complete removal of the cause of the offense.

3. Understand the *process of forgiveness.*

   a. When there is unforgiveness, known or unknown, the devil can attack.

   b. Someone has to assume the guilt, whether they are guilty or not.

   c. Enforce the victory of the cross by the innocent one taking the guilt to the cross.

   d. Confess with your mouth the victory of Jesus over guilt and blame.

Chapter Five

Principle IV - Cutting Soul Ties

Generational ties are inherited. They can be negative and will put a constant pull on you if they are not cut. Soul ties form from relationships with another person and can also hinder your destiny. A non-destiny soul tie is a relationship with someone who is not part of your purpose and destiny. Non-destiny soul ties must also be cut from you. These soul ties will hinder your destiny and correct soul ties of the future. A soul tie forms a link or connection between the ideas, beliefs, influences and behaviors of two or more people.

A soul tie
links you to another person

They can be like an albatross or dead weight to keep you in an old atmosphere and limitation. An atmosphere is the condition you are living in. It can be created by yourself or by others, but you choose to live in it. The atmosphere can be positive conditions or negative conditions. An atmosphere is your belief system and lifestyle you choose to live in. If it keeps you in the past, it will hinder your advancement and keep you from conquering your future. Discernment of relationships is crucial because some soul ties are positive and push you to your future as a sailboat with a full sail of wind.

Chapter Six

Principle V - Getting Permission and Pattern of Leaving from God

Genesis 31

At first, Jacob did not leave correctly. He followed all the wrong Principles of Leaving. He was afraid to face his father-in-law because he did not want a confrontation. He did not want to stand up for his rights and tell Laban that God had spoken to him to return to Bethel, the land of his father. In leaving a situation, circumstance, time, season or place, we need to be bold and declare the will of God for our leaving.

Boldly declare the will of God for your leaving

A declaration and seed of purpose must be released into the atmosphere. This declaration is three fold. First, it is for the ears of the evil spirits of darkness. Second, it is to declare that Almighty God has spoken. Third, it gives presence to the will of God that you have His approval to be released to leave.

Jacob did not do this. He left secretly without telling anyone. The proper etiquette of protocol for leaving was not carried out. The soul ties were not cut; therefore, the enemy had a legal right to pursue.

We cut a soul tie by the sword of the spirit. We first pray the prayer of forgiveness for entering a non-destiny soul tie. Then we take the sword of the spirit and cut the tie. Jacob did not carry out the blessings of leaving.

A generational blessing is very important for the success of the future. It is a blessing spoken over the next generation. The blessing should be spoken by someone in authority who can speak for God. Jacob spoke the blessing of God over his children before he died. Jesus was a prophet, and He spoke blessings over all generations to follow after Him.

Genesis 31:20 tells us Jacob stole away, unknown to Laban. The word *unknown* means the heart-felt feelings. It refers to the center or the heart of a thing with phrases such as: my heart goes out to someone, the heart and soul of a thing, or his heart is in the right place. Even though Laban was a deceiver, he still had rights to the proper leaving of his daughters. By leaving without notice, Jacob wounded the heart of Laban.

When you leave incorrectly, you can wound and hurt people. An offense has been committed and someone's rights have been violated. This gives the enemy a legal right to pursue and attack. When you leave without permission from God, an offense is committed. A stronghold of hurt is set up and you have violated God's will and purpose for those involved. If God has not given you permission to leave, then you can shipwreck your life.

In Acts 27:10, Paul told the captain not to leave port because it wasn't the right time. They did not believe Paul and set sail anyway. The ship wrecked and the cargo was lost.

It is a correct pattern regarding our forefathers to successfully leave the past by asking forgiveness of all our past failures, things known and unknown.

Part Two

Entering

Chapter One

Principle I - Getting the Right Seed

The most important part of entering is positioning yourself for the original intent of God. What has God planned for you? What has God predetermined for your life? What the seed produces, you walk out. Entering is entering into the life of the seed. Entering is the beginning of life. Life comes from the seed. Seed comes forth out of a desire. Everything begins with a desire and ends with a tree of life. Going from the beginning to the ending is called the journey, the process of life, the walk of life or the path of life. Journeying through life can be easy or it can be difficult. It all depends on the choices you make.

Man is a tri-part person. Desire can originate from any of these three parts: body, soul or spirit. A desire is a longing, passion, lust, or craving for something. So which part of man is in control? Each part can determine the seed you receive. The seed you receive is the gateway to entering. Desire reaches out and pulls the seed either from the kingdom of darkness whose head is Satan, or from the kingdom of light whose head is

45

God. The great principle of life comes from Genesis 8:22, which states that as long as earth remains, seedtime and harvest will not cease. You always reap what you sow.

You eat the fruit of your lips and become what you plant

Your future always comes from your past. You determine your future by the seeds you plant.

Entering right is critical. It is like the saying, "You only have one chance to make a good first-time impression." Once you have planted the seed, you have given life to the seed. If the seed is not from God, then it must be uprooted or brought to an end.

The process of life is simultaneous, dying and maturing. The dying is the process of bringing death to all the seeds we have given life to that did not originate from God's purpose and destiny for us. This process can be painful and long if we try to hang on to our own ways. The maturing is developing the seeds we have planted that originated from the intent of God for our lives. This process can be peaceful and short if we surrender quickly to the way of God or the path that God predetermined for us to walk in.

Principle I – Getting the Right Seed

Sometimes we enter into the life of a seed that is a lie, and we are damned. The seeds of tradition, the seeds of religion, and any negative seed will start our life off course. We must have zero tolerance at the beginning (the Entering), or as we journey through life, our destiny becomes off target.

Jesus is the way, the truth and the life. If we receive the wrong seed, it creates a wrong path. Then we are not in unity with God. We walk outside the full potential He has designed for our lives. We walk outside of His grace and love for us. He then starts the dying process of the wrong seed. Just as Eve ate in the Garden of Eden, we eat the fruit of our lips that we have produced — whether it be good or bad.

The reason for so much turmoil, hardships and disappointments in life is that our beginnings are wrong. The beginnings are not from the seed of purpose, but from our own desires and plans. The beginnings are created out of our soulish desires. God has planned our lives for us so that life can be a joy. Purpose protects us from doing good things at the expense of doing what is right. The problem is that many people are trying to seed their future from the experiences of the past instead of seed from the throne room.

Seed your future
from the throne room...
not from the past

This happens because we fail to bring proper closures to the past as we discussed in Principle V in Part One. Getting the right seed is critical for your future because your future is determined by what you plant today.

Your future is NOW!

Example - Luke 21:31-33. Jesus looked into the future and saw Peter's future. Jesus warned Peter that he would deny Him three times. Peter looked into the past and saw his experiences. He had acted boldly and had walked on water. Peter spoke his future based on his past instead of the spoken words of Jesus, so he failed. We cannot speak our future based on our past. We must go into the spirit realm and get our future and declare it in the present so we will have a future.

Chapter Two

Principle II - Right Attitude

You must enter with the right attitude. Attitude is how you feel or think about something, and the right attitude is critical to a successful life. Your attitude is either negative or positive. A negative attitude is from the kingdom of darkness and will keep you in a realm of limitation and failures. A negative attitude causes you to look through the eyes of darkness and into the defeated realm. This is the spirit of facade and is part of the lie. This attitude keeps you out of the realm of possibility and potential and causes you to think you cannot do something or you do not have the ability to do it. You look through the mask of facade and see everything in a wrong view. Your perception is distorted, and you will end up being deceived. You will think in a different way than how God thinks.

A positive attitude is from the Kingdom of Light. Light always conquers and dispels darkness. Light always triumphs over darkness. A positive attitude keeps you in the realm of possibility and potential. A positive attitude links you with God in

His unlimited ability. Attitude is a realm of victory and success which causes you to think you can do it. I am able to do it. I will do it.

I can do all things through Christ which strengtheneth me. Philippians 4:13

We must have the attitude of a fresh start, a new beginning. This creates joy in us to give us strength to start new and fresh. It also creates an excitement and expectancy within us as a level of faith enabling us to enter a new beginning.

Chapter Three

Principle III - Right Mindset

We must enter with a right mindset. How you think determines your success. You must see yourself as God sees you. A false mindset will cause you to see yourself as Satan sees you. God saw Gideon as a mighty warrior, a mighty man of valor, a great leader and deliverer of Israel (Judges 6:11-16).

Gideon saw himself as poor, little and insignificant. When you enter into the life of a seed from God, you have to align your thinking with the truth of the seed. When you enter into the life of the seed from God, you are entering into His ability and His anointing. You become one with Him, and have the mind of God and think His thoughts.

Romans 12:2 tells us we are transformed by the renewing of our minds. The definition of the word *renewing* here means to restore to a previous condition. There are only two conditions of the mind; one is before the fall of man and the other, after the fall of man. God wants us to renew our minds to think like Adam before he fell. We are to enter this mindset and walk as one with God as Adam did. We cannot walk one with God if we walk in the mindset of the fallen Adam. This fallen mindset tells us to do our own will even while God wants us to walk in His prepared steps for our lives.

The Bible tells us,

As a man thinketh in his heart, so is he...
Proverbs 23:7 (NKJV)

The word *thinketh* means door posts as a gatekeeper. As we think, we pass through a door or gate and enter into the new thought or decision. As we go through the door or gate, we enter into a new view, new surroundings, and a new atmosphere. This new mindset will cause us to walk out and become the intent of the thought. We are today what we thought and spoke yesterday. We will become tomorrow what we think and speak today. Therefore, the way we think determines our destiny.

Our thoughts
determine our destiny

Chapter Four

Principle IV - Close the Gate

As we enter the gate of a new seed, new thought or decision from God, we must close the door of our past thoughts and decisions so we cannot retreat or go back. Getting the seed from God was discussed in Principle I (Part Two). Some peoples' lives are like a revolving door. They have the "in and out syndrome" because they do not close the gate of the past.

Are you:
- up and down like a yo-yo?
- hot and cold like a steam engine?
- positive one day and negative the next day?
- Happy and joyous one day, then sad and discouraged the next?

What is the difference between Lot's wife and the prodigal son? They both started on a journey to a place of God's provision. Lot's wife looked back to the past. The lure of the past beckoned to her and she looked back. She did not close the gate of the past. The past consumed her and she turned into a pillar of salt. She was preserved in that condition. When we look back, we become mesmerized in that state. The Bible tells us not to look back. Jesus said, if man looks back, he is not fit for this kingdom of God (Luke 9:62). Our focus can be in the wrong direction. We are to continue looking and going forward to the future.

The prodigal son did not look back, but continued his journey to the Father's House. He received his blessing and reward. He looked forward to his Father's house.

Looking back causes us to remain in the past, while God's presence is on the present and future. When we look back, we become cold, down, and out of God's presence. This is the reason we are hot, cold, up, down, in and out.

**Look forward,
not backward**

Chapter Five

Principle V - Change

Change is imminent. One cannot enter the life of a new seed and not change. If a butterfly stayed in the stage of a cocoon, it would never change into a beautiful butterfly; the same need to change is with man. If man does not change, he will never be of the full stature of Jesus Christ He desires (Ephesians 4).

God made man into three parts: spirit, soul and body. After the fall of man into sin, He made the body to automatically grow, mature, and then to age and die. However, He also gave man the ability to mature and develop his soul and spirit. The Bible says that we can be a baby, a child, or a mature son.

The enemy of darkness deceives man so that he has no desire for change. As long as we stay an immature baby in spirit, we cannot be a threat to the devil. We cannot be a true example and light to the world or advance the Kingdom of God without change. Refusing to change is against God's order and plan. The devil covers it up as insignificant, but to God it is rebellion.

Paul tells us a baby has to stay on milk and can never become a full heir of God's blessings. He will remain a servant while always needing to be cared for. God wants to mature us and develop us into His character and full stature. We are changed into God's image from glory to glory (II Corinthians 3:18).

Chapter Six

Principle VI - War Over Seed

When we enter the life of the new seed or have entered into a new season of God, the devil comes immediately to steal the seed (Mark 4:15). Jesus was no exception (Matthew 3:17 and 4:1-11). Jesus was being baptized by John and God spoke from heaven, "This is my beloved son." Immediately after the baptizing, Satan came and tried to steal the seed from Jesus. Satan said to Jesus, "*If* you be the Son of God..." He was trying to get Jesus to doubt what God had just spoken to Him.

The three main weapons the devil uses are fear, doubt, and impatience. One of the definitions of *fear* is to take flight. When fear comes, it causes faith to take flight. Fear is a spirit from the devil to stop us from advancing, changing, or entering into something new or to change.

Fear
makes faith take flight

Doubt is a milder, more compromising word than the stronger word of unbelief. Doubt brings us out of the arena of faith of "now action" into the arena of "potential/future action." This is a wavering and questioning of the present so action will be put off to the future. Doubt can keep you from the present time and season of God.

Impatience causes us to leave or give up before the desired end result God wants to achieve. Impatience is a killer of endurance or waiting on God. God's creation testifies to this because nothing coming from a seed, whether plant, animal or human life, is produced or developed overnight. Life produced from a seed takes time, so do not abort life before maturity.

The same principle applies to a spiritual seed. We can abort the life and future of the seed by giving up. As long as we do not throw in the towel and become a quitter, there is always hope and potential for victory. Paul commanded Timothy to make war over his future.

This charge I commit unto thee, son Timothy, according to the prophecies which

went before on thee, that thou by them mightest war a good warfare; 1 Timothy 1:18

He received prophecies (words, seeds) from the throne room of God about his future. As already stated, your future is determined by the seeds you plant. Paul was instructing Timothy that he was responsible to guard and protect the seeds he had received so his future would be what God had planned for him. So, let's make war with the thief.

Mark 4 gives us the example of the enemies of the seed. We must follow the pattern of Jesus in dealing with the devil over stealing the seed. Jesus rebuked the devil with the Word. We must rebuke the devil by using the Word of God.

War over your seed!

Part Three

Biblical Examples of Leaving and Entering

Chapter One

Times and Seasons

Ecclesiastes 3:1 - To everything there is a season, a time for every purpose under heaven.

Times and seasons demand a correct pattern of Leaving and Entering to be successful. We need the spirit of Issachar to accurately discern the beginning and ending of the seasons of God.

And of the children of Issachar, *which were men* that had understanding of the times, to know what Israel ought to do; the heads of them *were* two hundred; and all their brethren *were* at their commandment.

I Chronicles 12:32

If we fail to discern the ending of a season, we will delay our entering into the new season. This will cause us to be late in receiving the benefits of the new season. It will put us behind others who entered on time.

God is saying there is, first of all, purpose. Purpose is the will of God, His desire and plans, what He wants to happen. Purpose is the reason for being, the reason for our existence. Everything that is created or exists first starts with purpose. God also is saying that purpose has a season and a time for existence. Time has past, present and future. If we do not understand Leaving and Entering, we can miss the purpose that God created.

The purposes of God are for the benefits and blessings of man. If we fail to properly discern the time and season of the purpose, then we fail to receive the benefits and blessings of the purpose. Purpose is either delayed or lost. Our future is determined by what we do in the present. When we live in the past instead of the present, then the future becomes our present, and we will not be ready for it. We also will not have the benefits and blessings of God for the present because we are still in the past.

God in His infinite wisdom did not create one long season or time period in His Redemptive Plan for fallen man. He established seasons and gave them a time frame to accomplish their purpose. This enables man to set short-term goals and give him a sense of accomplishing a task rather than having a daily and endless routine. God chose, for our benefit, not to restore everything at once. This causes us to go through the process of life to teach us a lesson. Adam remained only a short time in the garden.

Times and Seasons

Issachar means: He will bring a reward. When we know what God wants and we do it, He will reward and bless us. If we don't want what God wants, we may never achieve the fullness of the benefits of the season. Also God lifts His anointing from the previous season and rests His anointing on the new season. If we have not left the previous season, we will work in dead works or works of the flesh trying to produce results. This is the work of the spirit of religion.

When an individual or a group of people decide to remain in a season after it ends, they become locked into a time era. This is the work of an independent spirit. It is definitely not the will of God to be isolated and independent from the rest of the body.

We fail in God's purpose to advance the generational blessing from one generation to the next. Instead of advancing their input of purpose in technology, spiritual revelation, and knowledge, they impart the same old things of the past. God designed the seasons and filled them with His purposes. Why then do we rebel against His wishes? We cannot please Him and we can never walk in oneness with Him. We will always remain outside of the Holy of Holies or the throne room of God.

We will continue to eat old bread because we will not have a clue of what God is saying and doing today. We remain a relic of the past. God gives us natural seasons so we are constantly reminded of changing from one season to another season. There are natural things that happen in Entering and natural things that happen in the Leaving of a season. So we have no excuse for not discerning His spiritual things.

Any baggage we have, any influence of the world, or any effects and limitations of the kingdom of darkness will be carried into the new season if we fail to properly leave the old. When a runner enters a new race, he immediately removes all the old clothes and puts on his new racing clothes. Not only does he trade old clothes, but he also leaves behind the effects of the old race. The failures, defects, limitations, and attitudes are left behind. We enter the new season with expectancy, new hope, new attitudes, new strategy and new goals. This will cause us to plan for our success.

Chapter Two

Our Future

God has planned our future as we stated in Principle I of Entering (Part Two). God tells us in Jeremiah 29:11 that He has plans and purposes to give us peace and prosperity. Ephesians 1:11 tells us He predestined us according to His purpose. God has planned our lives for success, prosperity and happiness. However, if we never seek Him to find out what He has planned for our lives, then we may never find success, prosperity and happiness. It is like playing Russian roulette and becomes a hit-or-miss lifestyle.

God has planned our journey through life, but those plans are in the spirit realm because God is Spirit. We have to enter the Throne Room of God by the Holy Spirit to receive what He has planned for our lives.

We then bring the seeds out of the spirit realm and declare them in the natural realm. We set them as our goals to achieve. Goals should be the revealed will of God for our lives. They are prophetic insights to our future. God says everyone should prophesy. We prophesy our future and establish it as our goals.

Your plans for the future are in the Throne Room

We can never become one with God if He is walking in one path and we are walking on another path. We are living our lives in rebellion unless we find out what He has planned for us. It is a deception of the devil if we think we are not in rebellion. It is our responsibility as stewards over our purposes to find out our plans from God and take the necessary action to implement them. Goals keep us on the right path. Goals keep us looking into the future until restoration of all things is complete in us.

Chapter Three

The Lord's Prayer

The Lord 's Prayer is the model prayer. Jesus gave us this prayer, not to just repeat, but to follow its principles to bring success like He achieved. This prayer is an example of Leaving and Entering. We are to leave each day and enter into the next day. Jesus instructed us to get our daily bread. Bread is our daily word from heaven, not the natural bread we eat. Jesus is telling us to get our new instructions from heaven, as each new day dawns, so we can be successful. God has already planned the steps we are to take each day.

In Matthew 6:34 Jesus tells us to be not anxious for tomorrow because He already has it planned for us. Jesus is the bread of life, the manifested word, the way, so we call upon Him each new day. God's plan is for us to end each day (Leaving) and to enter into each new day (Entering) what He has already prepared for us to do. We close out each day with the prayer of forgiveness for our failures and shortcomings for any way we missed the mark or goal for the day.

Chapter Four

Shabbat

God gave man the plan for his success. Part of the plan for success includes instructions to end each week and to begin the next week. To be successful, we are to leave each week and to enter the new week in God's order. The Shabbat Table is the altar of God. God ordered man to bring his family to the table at the end of the week for a special meal. Shabbat means to cease. The old week is to cease and be left behind. The candles are lit. The fresh bread and the special meal are ready; however, it is the principle of the special occasion that is so important to man.

God is acknowledged and thanked for His blessings. Prayers of thanksgiving, cleansing and forgiveness, and blessings are prayed. At the close of Shabbat a special ceremony of Havdalah is observed. Havdalah means separation. The old week and the new week are separated. A prayer is prayed to prepare for entering the new week. The new week is entered with an expected view of the next Shabbat and not of the old one. This is God's plan for all mankind and not only for Jews.

Chapter Five

Prodigal Son

When we accept Jesus as our Savior and enter into a relationship with God, we must leave the ways of the world and our old lifestyle. The prodigal son left the old lifestyle he was living to enter his father's house. He left the pig pen and living like the world for a much better life. There is always a prerequisite of entering into God's promises. There is first the Leaving and then the Entering.

In II Corinthians 6:14-18, God tells us to come out from unbelievers and separate from their ways of ungodliness. In Ephesians 4:22, God tells us to leave the former way of life and enter the new life of the spirit. The prodigal son is our example of this pattern. One can see the old lifestyle of the degradation of the world compared to the blessing of the Father's house. There was provision, inheritance, love, music and position of authority in the Father's house.

We have a choice today, blessings or curses. I choose the Father's House, the Kingdom of God over the kingdom of Satan.

Part Four

Major Events
in
Our Lives

Chapter One

Education

There are those whom I call "Professional Education Addicts." They are always searching for a profession where they feel they can fit or be happy with, but they never seem to find it. Therefore, many years are wasted while searching for the right professions.

Then there are those who fall short and drop out of school too early. They really never had a vision for their future. Also there are those with a proper education according to their own desires and vision. All the above enter into the work force without following the Principles of Leaving and Entering.

The devil is no respecter of persons and will attack anyone whether rich or poor, educated or uneducated, in every nationality of the world. The Bible says he comes to kill, steal and destroy. This includes every part of our body and everything related to our journey through life. Our health, finances, family and relationships are a target for his schemes and devices. A major weapon Satan uses is regret.

> 8For even if I made you sorry with my letter, I do not regret it: though I did regret it. For I perceive that the same epistle made you sorry, though only for a while.
> 10For godly sorrow produces repentance *leading* to salvation, not to be regretted: but the sorrow of the world produces death.
>
> II Corinthians 7:8,10 (NKJ)

Regret is pain of mind on account of something done or experienced in the past, to mourn loss, to feel remorseful or troubled over something that has happened. Regret is also defined as a negative conscious and emotional reaction to personal past acts and behavior. When we look back on our education choices in a negative view of not being enough or not being correct training, disappointment can weigh so heavy on our minds. The load can seem so unbearable that negative actions and even suicide thoughts can grip us. Judas is a good example of this. The regret of betraying Jesus was so great, he took his own life into his hands and committed suicide.

Guilt and shame stem from regret. Once regret starts its downward spiral, each step leads into a deeper pit. Unless we look up out of the pit and see a way out of it, and then come out of it and

Education

leave it behind, we will remain hopeless. Hopelessness leads one into depression. When we look back, it leads to regret and regret causes discontentment; then discontentment steals our joy. When joy is depleted, our strength to continue our life's journey and reach our destiny is weakened. The correct way to leave our education is to be thankful for the level we achieved.

As we enter the work force, we are to be thankful for the position and job we have. Paul said to be content in the state we are in. This does not mean we should not have a vision for climbing the corporate ladder or higher goals. Once we have left our level of education, the enemy's plan is to cause us to look back with regret. To be successful, we cannot entertain these thoughts. We must leave our educational level with thankfulness, ask for forgiveness if we've fallen short, and never look back with regret.

Chapter Two

Marriage

The reason for so many divorces is failure to apply the Principles of Leaving and Entering. There are certain prayers that need to be prayed before the marriage ceremony is performed. Soul ties need to be broken with former relationships. If pre-marital sex was committed by either party, a special prayer to leave correctly needs to be prayed. (Refer to Prayers to Be Prayed in Chapter Five.)

If there was a previous marriage from either partner, then you need to leave the old marriage correctly. Without properly leaving your lifestyles, behavior patterns, and the negative side of your personality traits, you can never achieve the oneness in marriage that God desires and has planned for. Therefore, you will never achieve the full power and blessings of marriage.

Chapter Three

Death

We never consider that our final closure or death could leave a curse on our loved ones. When those left behind do not follow the Principles of Leaving and Entering, they can experience damaging emotional or physical handicaps. This happens to a lot of people who do not properly process the death of a loved one. There is a natural process of grief that is good for us, but there is also a spirit of grief from the devil that is not good for us.

The process of leaving the grave site is to acknowledge that God is sovereign. We cannot question God as to why this happened. To question God is to rebel against His authority as God. This can lead to the spirit of grief overpowering us and giving the enemy the right to continue to attack us. This will hinder us from going into our future and finishing our purpose. Some people remain in this state of grief, never achieving the fullness of their lives.

We are to release our loved one into the hands of God. Trying to hold on to them will cause a part of them to remain with us and bring a constant reminder of them that can bring damaging effects to our bodies. The bonding of a friend or family member is a powerful thing. This physical and emotional bonding has to be released or you will continue to carry part of the deceased around with you. This will create an unhealthy state of being for you.

I do not believe you should keep an urn of ashes in your possession. This is not a proper release of the deceased. You are still trying to hold onto someone when God has closed their time to live on the earth.

This is not saying to forget them, but your life must continue to fulfill your destiny. Releasing them to God will bring a closure to this part of your life so that you can properly enter into the next season of your life without them.

King David was a good example of this. While his son was sick, he fasted, prayed, and mourned for him. After he died, he stopped mourning. He washed himself, went and worshiped God, and ate. The servants questioned him and David said, "I now prepare myself to meet him on the other side. I can go to him, but he cannot come to me." Do not allow the death of a loved one to lock you up and keep you a prisoner of the past. Even if we feel or have a thought that God has shown injustice or not been fair to allow

Death

someone's life to be short, we still have to forgive Him. Forgiveness is a basic principle of the plan of success. After David's son died, David worshiped God.

Chapter Four

Closing

Leaving and Entering is a pattern given to man from God to show us how to transition through life successfully.

From the moment of pregnancy to the closing of the grave, this pattern is to be followed. The way we enter this life and the way we leave this life determines our eternal life. The quality and success of living between birth and death depends on how well we leave and enter life's seasons and processes. Without this pattern we can become locked into time with our mindsets, and we will always be in the past because we never transition into the present and will never achieve the future.

Abraham (the father of us all) had to leave and enter as he journeyed through life, and God's blessings were upon him. Jesus also used the pattern of Leaving and Entering and He finished His purpose on earth, pleasing God. God exalted Him and gave Him a name above all names.

Chapter Five

Invocation and Benediction

Invocation is the opening or beginning of a service of worship. Benediction is the closing of a service of worship. I ask the question, "When does a worship service begin and when does it end?" The normal or logical answer would be, "It begins with the designated time to begin. Also it closes at the designated time to close."

Is this the way God planned for us to worship? What is God's plan for Leaving and Entering a worship service? If we look at the pattern of Shabbat that God gave us, we will find His plan for Leaving and Entering a worship service.

The Romans stripped Christianity of its Jewish origins and created a fake pattern of Leaving and Entering a worship service. Then Constantine compromised Christianity with pagan practices and forced the Christians to conform to them. The Church accepted the decrees and made them part of church practices.

The Jews did not bow to these compromising decrees but kept the ways of God. The Jews use a special service called Havdalah to transition from Shabbat to the new week. Havdalah means to separate. This ceremony brings an ending to Shabbat and prepares the beginning of the next Shabbat. The Jews enter into the new week with an expectancy of another Shabbat. They immediately start preparing for the next Shabbat.

Expectancy is a type of faith. They have started building their faith for the next Shabbat. We have lost this excitement and expectancy in the church. We live and do as we please all week and go to worship service in all kinds of mindsets, attitudes and with sin in our lives. Most people never achieve God's best for their lives simply because they do not follow His Principles of Leaving and Entering.

In Matthew 5:13-16, Jesus said we are the salt and the light of the world. We should live our lives during the week in such a manner that we are a praise to the Lord Jesus Christ. We should have the same attitude as the Jew concerning the expectancy and excitement of the new Shabbat.

I believe the Invocation should be held immediately after the Benediction. We should praise God all week. Then at the closing of the worship service we should reach a level of worship so that we come face to face with God's Glory. It is in His presence that we are changed from Glory to Glory.

Many people are not changed because they have never entered the atmosphere of the worship service. Their minds are wandering. They are either thinking of what happened during the week or what they plan to do the next week. Dr. John Looper, president of Restoration Fellowship International in Cleveland, Tennessee, has a powerful statement, "Wherever you are, then be there." If our minds are wandering, we cannot soak up the presence of God. We cannot receive the inspired Word of God that changes our lives.

The Jews do not have this problem because they have already entered into preparation and a mindset for the next Shabbat. They are already planning how to make this Shabbat better than the last one. The Jews did not allow the Greco-Roman decrees and teaching to influence them. They kept the practices given to them by God.

We followed the decrees of the Greco-Roman rulers. We forget about church and God after the Benediction until the Invocation of the next worship service. During the time period between worship services, we are often influenced by the devil more than we are influenced by God. It is time for us to rethink our Invocation and

Benediction. The pattern of Leaving and Entering is one of God's greatest plans of success for our lives. We need to live every day by the Principles of the pattern.

Chapter Six

Prayers to Be Prayed

Prayer of Leaving

Heavenly Father, I thank You for all the blessings You provided for me in this past season of my life. Forgive me for any way I have failed You, missed the mark, allowed any wrong thinking, or have been influenced in any way by the spirit of darkness. I now take the sword of the Spirit and cut any non-destiny activities or non-destiny soul ties away from myself. Thank You that I am forgiven, washed, and made clean by the blood of Jesus. I am free from any bondages of the devil and his influence.

Prayer of Entering

Heavenly Father, I thank You for the new season You have called me into. I enter this season by faith and pray the life of this new seed will flourish in me. I confess with my mouth that I will fulfill the purpose of this seed and season. I enter this new season with joy and expectation. I pray I will fulfill this new mandate on time, with excellence and with accuracy in Jesus' Name.

Prayer before Marriage

Heavenly Father, I thank You for leading me to the right mate. I prepare my heart to enter into an eternal covenant with __(Name)__ .

(If there has been sex outside of marriage or you have been married before, you need to say the following prayer.)

Father, forgive me for sexual immorality and ungodly covenants. I send back to (Name) anything I received from __him/her__ cleansed by the blood. I bring back to me anything __he/she__ received from me cleansed by the blood of Jesus. All soul ties are broken and I am now cleansed and made whole again for my future mate. I thank You for a happy, successful marriage.

Prayer at Death

Heavenly Father, I thank You for allowing
_____ to be my _____(wife, husband,
mother, father, son, daughter, friend, etc.). I do not
question the loss or your sovereign will. I release
_____ now into Your hands for safe
keeping. Thank You, Lord that a spirit of grief
cannot overtake my life because I have given
him/her to You and I have brought closure to this
part of my life. I break all soul ties with _____
and enter this new season of my life with peace.
I will not live in the past, but commit my future
into Your will and purpose. I ask You to plant a
new seed of purpose in my heart and that my
purpose may be fulfilled successfully.

Prayer of Salvation

Jesus, I believe You died on the cross for me. I believe You shed Your blood to cleanse me from all sin. Forgive me for all my sin, my failures and shortcomings. I thank You for forgiving me and cleansing me. I now ask You, Jesus to come into my heart and dwell in me.

Thank You that I am now born again and I make You (Jesus) the Lord of my life. I will live for You. I choose to walk away from the path of sin and my alliance with Satan. I now begin a new life with God.

Emphasis Statements

non-destiny activities
non-destiny relationships
page 3

Beginnings
determine endings
page 10

Religion
deceives man into thinking
he has left the kingdom of darkness
page 15

A religious spirit will cause us
to desire a denomination or a false religion
more than an encounter with Truth
page 15

The second Principle of Leaving
is to acknowledge
God is sovereign
Page 21

You become
what you are connected to
page 25

Enforce the victory of the cross
Page 26

Forgiveness closes the door
Page 32

A soul tie
links you to another person
page 37

Boldly
declare the will of God
for your leaving
page 39

You eat the fruit of your lips
and become what you plant
page 46

Seed your future
from the throne room...
not from the past
page 48

Your future is NOW!
Page 48

Our thoughts
determine our destiny
page 52

Look forward,
not backward
page 54

Fear
makes faith take flight
page 58

War over your seed!
Page 59

Your plans for the future
are in the Throne Room
page 68

Index

Made in the USA
Lexington, KY
07 June 2015